THE GOLDEN COMPASS™

THE MODERN WORLD

THE WORLD OF THE GOLDEN COMPASS

CLIVE GIFFORD

SCHOLASTIC

Scholastic Children's Books
Euston House, 24 Eversholt Street,
London NW1 1DB, UK
A division of Scholastic Ltd
London – New York – Toronto – Sydney – Auckland
Mexico City – New Delhi – Hong Kong

Editorial Director: Lisa Edwards
Project Manager: Neil Kelly
Project Editor: Laura Milne
Designer: Aja Bongiorno

ISBN-10: 1 407 10329 6
ISBN-13: 978 1407 10329 7

Contents

Introduction

Welcome to the amazing world of *The Golden Compass*, a place where
magic, mystery, beauty and danger are never far away. It is a world that
exists in a parallel universe, and although it is similar to the Earth we know, it also
contains the most extraordinary people, places and creatures. Throughout this world
adults and children live their lives guided and helped by their dæmons – a part of a person's
soul in the form of an animal, which lives outside of their body.

The continents are familiar, but there are many different lands and kingdoms. Majestic airships ferry
passengers between the ancient cities of Oxford and London in the country of Brytain, while
ships voyage east across the great, churning sea to the rocky shores of Norroway.
The port town of Trollesund in Norroway is the gateway to the North, a region of hostile,
snow-covered wastes, giant forests and spectacular ice kingdoms. Occupied by Tartar warriors and
Samoyed fur traders, it is also home to ferocious, intelligent, armoured Ice Bears. Beautiful, ageless
witches fly through the Northern skies, and at the very top of the world, where the
gap between the universes is thin, the translucent aura of the Northern Lights
illuminates a mysterious city in the sky.

The world of *The Golden Compass* is home to peoples and creatures of great
bravery and ingenuity, but there are also dark forces at work.
A great conflict is brewing, and the fate of all the worlds in every
universe may depend on the actions of a young
girl named Lyra Belacqua...

Lyra

Twelve-year-old Lyra Belacqua is an adventurous, fiercely independent girl. Orphaned after her parents died in an airship accident, she was left in the care of the scholars of Jordan College in Oxford, Brytain, by her uncle, Lord Asriel. Lyra is skilled at telling stories and her curiosity often gets her into trouble. But she is also loyal and trustworthy, and will risk her own safety to protect those she cares about. The arrival at Jordan of the mysterious Mrs Coulter, and the disappearance of Lyra's friend Roger Parslow, sets the feisty orphan off on an epic quest.

Lyra's constant companion is her dæmon, Pantalaimon – or Pan for short. Pan is more cautious than Lyra, and helps to curb her impulsive nature. Although they often argue, the love between Lyra and her dæmon is clear to see. Throughout their adventures, they provide each other with support and comfort. And when Lyra is at her lowest, Pan reminds her that, while he is there, she is never truly alone.

When Lyra leaves Oxford to begin her travels, the Master of Jordan College presents her with an alethiometer - an extraordinary truth-telling device also known as the Golden Compass. Lyra soon discovers she has a natural ability to use the alethiometer. Her new-found skill proves to be invaluable as she visits strange new lands and encounters amazing characters along the way.

At Jordan College, Lyra's happiest times are spent playing on the roofs with her friend, the servant boy Roger Parslow (left). When Roger disappears, Lyra embarks on a quest that leads her to the frozen wastes of the North. On her journey, she falls under the protection of the Western Gyptians (above), a fierce tribe of sea-faring warriors and traders.

The scholars at Jordan College try to educate Lyra and teach her politeness and good manners, but she is determined not to become a well-mannered lady. As she says to Roger, "Nobody can make me a lady, not the Master, and Scholars and Porters combined, right?" But for all her unruliness, she is also brave, caring and exceptionally bright. Lyra's curiosity and impatience for new experiences propel her into situations; her desire to explore the off-limits Retiring Room at Jordan College, for example, enables Lyra to save Lord Asriel's life when Fra Pavel (pg 23) attempts to poison him. Lyra is is also entranced by the fascinating worlds described to her by the glamorous Mrs Coulter (pgs 18–19) when they dine together in Oxford. And when she accepts Mrs Coulter's offer to travel with her to London and become her assistant, it is the beginning of the greatest adventure of Lyra's young life.

Lyra's courage earns her the respect and loyalty of Iorek Byrnison, a fearsome, armoured Ice Bear. Lyra's ability to use her story-telling skills to outwit her enemies prompts Iorek to give her an appropriate nickname - Lyra Silvertongue.

Dæmons

In Lyra's world, part of a person's soul lives on the outside of their body. It takes the form of a dæmon – a talking animal spirit that accompanies a person through life. A child's dæmon can change shape, assuming all the forms that a child's unlimited potential inspires. But as a person gets older, their dæmon gradually settles into one form, according to their character and nature.

Far, far more than a pet or a close companion, dæmons are able to talk and act on behalf of their human. Dæmons and their humans are connected through an invisible bond of energy, which enables them to share each other's thoughts and feelings. If a person experiences a strong emotion or pain, so does their dæmon. This works the other way round as well, as Mrs Coulter finds out when her monkey-dæmon's paw is trapped in a window frame by Lyra.

Dæmons are usually the opposite gender to their human – for example, Lyra's dæmon, Pantalaimon, is male. When two friends greet each other, their dæmons will often nuzzle and stroke one another – but it is not considered appropriate to touch another person's dæmon. When a person dies, their dæmon fades away moments afterwards.

To people in Lyra's world, it is unthinkable to imagine life without a dæmon. If a person were to be separated from their dæmon, they would be seen as terribly mutilated.

Mrs Coulter's dæmon has settled in its final "adult" shape, taking the form of a Golden Monkey.

The dæmon of a Tartar warrior takes the form of a wolf (right).

Humans and their dæmons share an incredibly close connection which prevents the dæmon from roaming very far. If the bond of energy that links them is stretched too far, it causes them both extreme anguish and pain. Lyra experiences this when Pan is pulled away from her by Mrs Coulter's dæmon – the Golden Monkey – to teach her a lesson. Witches' dæmons, however, can roam much further than those belonging to ordinary humans. The armoured Ice Bears of Svalbard do not have dæmons – but some of them are envious of the human-dæmon relationship.

As a person grows older, their dæmon settles down into one animal form and cannot change. The form it takes usually reflects the person's character and personality. Lord Asriel's loyal servant Thorold, for instance, has a faithful dog as his dæmon, while the fierce Tartar warriors of the North all have wolves. The disreputable child-kidnappers known as the Gobblers, who try to capture Lyra in London at night, have foxes, wildcats or jackals as their dæmons.

Lord Asriel's snow-leopard dæmon, Stelmaria, has the same piercing blue eyes as her human (below).

The kindly Gyptian Ma Costa has a watchful, courageous hawk as her dæmon.

Pantalaimon

Lyra Belacqua's dæmon is called Pantalaimon, or Pan for short. He is her friend, confidante and closest companion. His most common shapes are his ferret, ermine and cat forms, but he has also been known to change into a bird, a mouse, a snake, a moth and even a frog.

Pan's cautious nature often helps to keep his impulsive human out of trouble. Lyra cannot help but speak her mind, whereas Pan often urges her to keep her thoughts to herself. While Lyra tends to rush into situations, her dæmon is often far more aware of danger. He is fearful for Lyra being caught and spanked, for instance, when she sneaks into the off-limits Retiring Room at Jordan College. On another occasion, he tries to persuade Lyra not to enter a mysterious trapper's hut in the North as he senses something bad inside – but she steps inside anyway.

Pantalaimon usually assumes his cat form when he is wary of possible danger.

Lyra's dæmon switches forms (left) in reaction to situations, changing from a moth to a small bird to a mouse. When roused, Pan may take the form of a snake or even a snow leopard to protect Lyra.

Pantalaimon often takes the form of a ferret (right).

Lyra often dismisses Pan's warnings and accuses him of cowardice, but he is simply trying to curb her adventurous nature for her own protection. Pan shows great bravery on many occasions, and he is decisive and quick to react. He comes to Lyra's rescue when Mrs Coulter's monkey-dæmon attempts to steal the alethiometer, changing into a bird to fly past and pluck the device from the dæmon's grasp.

The connection between Lyra and Pan is very strong, but Lyra stretches the bond of energy between them to the very limit when she seeks out the fearsome Ice Bear Iorek Byrnison in Trollesund. Pan refuses to approach Iorek, holding his ground as Lyra struggles her way closer to the bear. In the end, Pan gives in, but the agony Lyra and her dæmon suffer reduces them both to tears.

To Lyra, a life without Pan would be worse than death. The two of them may bicker and disagree on what to do in many situations, but they provide each other with constant love and support. Lyra's dæmon is always there to comfort her when she is at her lowest, giving her the strength to carry on even in the most desperate and dangerous situations.

Jordan College

 owering above the streets of Oxford are the spires and roofs of Jordan College. It is the oldest, grandest and most powerful of all the seats of learning in the city. The scholars of Jordan College study many subjects, including metaphysics and celestial geography. Jordan is also home to the spirited orphan Lyra Belacqua, and it is here that her story begins...

The Master is the head of Jordan College. When Lord Asriel left Lyra at the college as an infant, he entrusted her to the Master's care and protection. A learned man who is fond of Lyra, the Master warns her against leaving Oxford and travelling with Mrs Coulter. Before Lyra departs, he gives her a small bag containing a device called an alethiometer (pgs 14–15), but asks her to keep it safe and make sure that Mrs Coulter doesn't get hold of it. The Master believes that Lyra is the child described in an ancient prophecy who will bring an end to a great war that began thousands of years ago.

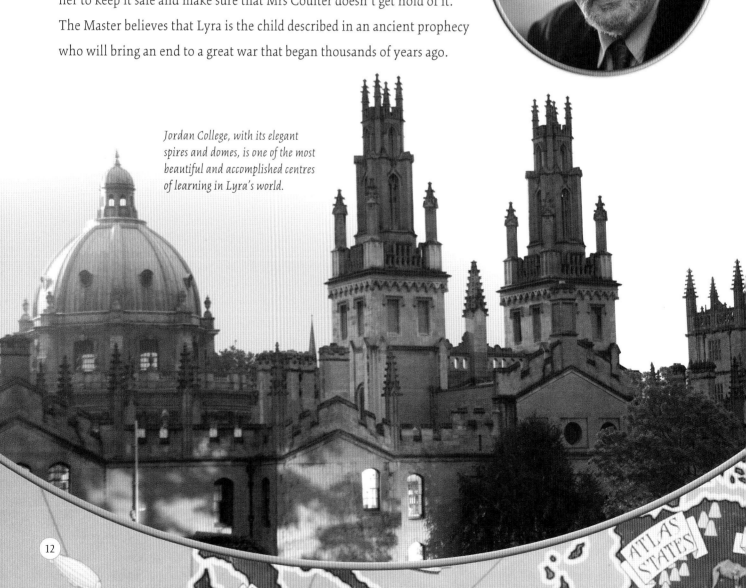

Jordan College, with its elegant spires and domes, is one of the most beautiful and accomplished centres of learning in Lyra's world.

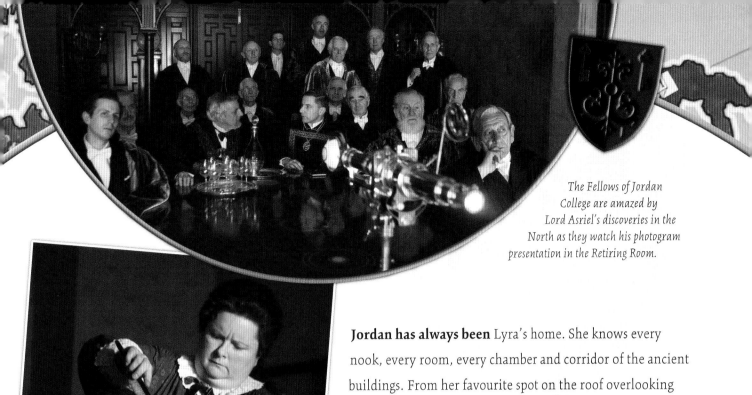

The Fellows of Jordan College are amazed by Lord Asriel's discoveries in the North as they watch his photogram presentation in the Retiring Room.

Jordan has always been Lyra's home. She knows every nook, every room, every chamber and corridor of the ancient buildings. From her favourite spot on the roof overlooking the Great Quad, she can spy most of Oxford. Although Lyra is high-born, most of her friends at the college are the children of the servants who work there. Lyra is looked after by the college's housekeeper, Mrs Lonsdale. Although she frequently tells Lyra off for misbehaving, Mrs Lonsdale cares for the lively child deeply.

Mrs Lonsdale combs Lyra's unruly hair in another unsuccessful attempt to make her more lady-like.

All the scholars at Jordan College are men. The most senior scholars – the Fellows – dine on plates of gold set on the High Table in the large Dining Hall. It is here that Lyra first meets Mrs Coulter. Close to the Dining Hall is the Retiring Room. This gloomily lit chamber is where the Master and other scholars go after dinner to relax or to talk about serious matters. It is off-limits to Lyra, but on one occasion she cannot resist creeping into the room. Hiding as the adults enter, she overhears Lord Asriel's tales of discovery in the North and his plan to travel to other worlds.

Concerned for Lyra, the Master watches as Mrs Coulter dazzles the amazed child with tales of armoured Ice Bears and exciting, far-away places.

13

The Alethiometer

Many years ago, Lord Asriel left a rare magical device with the Master of Jordan College. When Lyra prepares to leave Oxford for a new life in London, the Master decides that the precious, golden instrument should be given to her for safe-keeping. This special device is called an alethiometer, but its elegant design has also earned it another name – the Golden Compass. But while an ordinary compass always shows true North, the alethiometer's needle points to Truth itself.

The alethiometer looks like a beautifully carved compass or pocket watch. Its intricately inscribed cover opens to reveal a dial, at the centre of which are three hands and a needle. Around the dial's edge are 36 signs and symbols. Some of the symbols are animals, including a bull, a bee, a chameleon and a dolphin. Others show people like a lady, a baby, or objects such as an hourglass, a crucible, an anchor or a bolt of lightning.

Moving the hands of the alethiometer is easy, but knowing how to form a question and understand the answers is much more difficult. Each of the symbols can mean many things. The secrets of how to read and understand the device were guarded jealously in the past and modern scholars have found it impossible to learn. The wise and knowledgeable Gyptian elder Farder Coram (pgs 32–33) doubts there is anyone alive who has the skill.

There are three short hands and one long needle on the alethiometer's dial. To ask the device a question, the hands are turned by small knobs so that each points to a different symbol. Then, while the reader holds the question in their mind, the needle spins around the dial to reveal the answer.

The alethiometer gets its name from the Greek word, aletheia, meaning truth. When the Master gives Lyra the device, he tells her that it is a truth-telling machine.

Lyra finds that she has a unique ability to use the alethiometer. She is able to ask it a question, focus her mind and instinctively learn the truth. Lyra first uses the device to learn the fate of three Gyptian spies. Later, she uses it to find Iorek Byrnison's armour and to discover how Ragnar Sturlusson, the King of Svalbard (pgs 42–43), came to power.

To learn the fate of the Gyptian spies, Lyra selected the serpent, crucible and bee symbols (right) on the alethiometer's dial. The device's answer showed that they had suffered harm.

Lord Asriel

A respected Fellow of Jordan College, Lord Asriel is an eminent explorer and soldier. Stern and proud, he is also Lyra Belacqua's uncle. Too busy with his research and explorations to play a major role in Lyra's life, Asriel left the orphaned child in the care of the Fellows when she was a baby. He often hides his emotions, and has little patience. On his latest visit to Jordan, he appears ungrateful when Lyra foils a plot to poison him. Despite this, Lyra admires and respects her uncle.

When Asriel visits Jordan College, he is in need of money to continue his work. Twelve months previously, he had travelled to the kingdom of Svalbard and reached the magnetic North Pole. Asriel reveals to the Jordan Fellows his discovery of glowing particles from space called Dust, which flow into humans through their dæmons. He also explains his findings that the barrier between universes is very thin at the North Pole. With sufficient funding and a suitable source of energy, Asriel intends to break through the barrier and explore other worlds.

Lord Asriel is very focused and determined to succeed at all costs. He is also prepared to sacrifice others to achieve his aims. Asriel's dæmon is a sleek and powerful snow leopard named Stelmaria.

Taken at the North Pole, Asriel's photogram image shows Dust from space flowing into a man through his dæmon (near right).

After he secures funding for his trip, Asriel refuses Lyra's request to accompany him on his next journey to the North (far right).

Fra Pavel, a representative of the Magisterium is also present at Lord Asriel's presentation. He accuses Asriel of heresy, and is furious when the college council grant Asriel his funding. Asriel leaves Jordan shortly afterwards, stopping only for a brief conversation with Lyra in the college gardens. Lyra is eager to travel North with her exciting uncle and meet the Ice Bears of Svalbard, but he shatters her hopes. However, he does promise to bring her back a carved walrus tusk – a small consolation to Lyra.

After travelling to the North herself some time later, Lyra finds out that Asriel has been captured and imprisoned by Ragnar Sturlusson, the bear-king of Svalbard. She plans to rescue him, but it turns out that his jail is far from a cold, cramped stone cell. Instead, it is a luxurious ice-house filled with expensive furniture and sophisticated scientific instruments. Lord Asriel has been allowed to continue his work and to keep his aged servant, Thorold, who looks after Lyra and her friend, Roger Parslow, when they arrive. At first Asriel appears to be horrified to see them but quickly regains his cool. Lyra offers him the alethiometer, but it is of no interest to him. However, he is secretly pleased as Lyra has brought him the one thing he needs to complete his experiments...

Asriel's luxurious prison quarters in Svalbard contain useful instruments and equipment to enable him to carry out his research.

Mrs Coulter

Beautiful, powerful and enigmatic, Mrs Marisa Coulter is a woman of many talents. She is a scholar, Arctic explorer and socialite, and also holds a high-ranking position in the Magisterium – the organization that runs Lyra's world. Her elegant appearance, commanding voice and charming manner enable her to dazzle all who meet her. Whether she is addressing the sombre Fellows of Jordan College, dining in London high-society or trudging through the icy wastes of the North, Mrs Coulter is a person who always gets what she wants.

Lyra first meets Mrs Coulter when she is a guest at Jordan College. Over dinner, Mrs Coulter mesmerizes Lyra with tales of lands and peoples far from Oxford. The glamorous visitor appears to take an instant interest in the wilful child, and invites Lyra to come back with her to London. There, Lyra will have to study hard and learn subjects such as mathematics, navigation and celestial geography. But, if she does so, she will get the chance to join Mrs Coulter on an expedition to the North. Lyra is overjoyed at this exciting prospect – so long as Mrs Coulter is her teacher.

Marisa Coulter's dæmon (below right) is an attractive-looking, nameless monkey with golden fur. However, the Golden Monkey is also vicious, spiteful and dangerous. Mrs Coulter's dæmon is a reflection of the lady herself - her charming and beautiful appearance masks a ruthless and cruel nature.

Glamorous and strikingly beautiful, Mrs Coulter is a domineering presence at Jordan College (left). Her stylish, expensively furnished London home (above right) indicates her high status and power.

When Lyra leaves Oxford and goes to stay with Mrs Coulter in London, she is showered with new clothes and taken out for fine dinners. But a darker, more sinister side to Mrs Coulter's nature is soon revealed. The elegant woman has no problem causing Lyra pain by pulling Pan from her – stretching the bond between human and dæmon – in order to teach her a lesson. She also appears to be connected to the Gobblers (pgs 24–25) – the name given to the kidnappers responsible for abducting children in London and Oxford. Finally, she tries to steal Lyra's precious alethiometer. And when Lyra flees from the London apartment, Mrs Coulter and Fra Pavel release a pair of deadly spy-flies (pg 21) to find Lyra and retrieve the alethiometer.

Mrs Coulter and Lyra meet again at Bolvangar (pgs 40–41), a research station in the frozen North where the Gobblers send their victims. It is here that Mrs Coulter reveals to Lyra a number of well-kept secrets about her past – secrets which will forever change the nature of their relationship.

Although she saves Lyra from a terrible experiment at Bolvangar, Mrs Coulter is, in fact, in charge of the gruesome research that takes place at the Experimental Station.

Technology and Transport

Many amazing forms of technology and transportation are employed in Lyra's world. The main source of energy is anbaric power. This is similar to electricity in our world, but the means of generating it results in a glowing, flame-like light. Naptha – an oily substance – is also used as fuel in older lamps and heating systems.

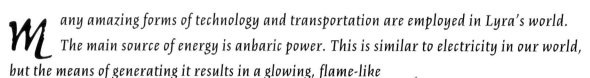

Photograms are three-dimensional images that are displayed using an intricate, hand-fashioned device called a spirit projector (right). The images are stored in special glass spheres which are inserted into the device and projected against a wall. At Jordan College, Lord Asriel uses a spirit projector during his presentation to the Master, the Fellows and Fra Pavel. His photogram images capture extraordinary scenes from his recent expedition to the North Pole.

In London, senior officials of the Magisterium travel around the sprawling metropolis in luxurious Magisterial carriages (left). Powered by glowing, anbaric energy, these speedy vehicles are a highly efficient form of transport.

The majestic scarlet and gold livery of the huge Magisterial sky ferry (right) reflects the power and status of the Magisterium – the organization that rules Lyra's world.

For long-distance travel, the preferred method of transport is by airship. These graceful craft are held aloft by hydrogen-filled balloons and powered by anbaric motors. Lyra Belacqua's first major journey – from Oxford to London – is aboard a Magisterial sky ferry. These magnificent, giant airships travel between different aerodromes, where they take-off and land. Powerful, wealthy institutions such as Jordan College have their own special facilities – the Great Quad at Jordan College is equipped with its very own sky-ferry terminal.

The water-faring Gyptian people sail along canals and waterways in homely barges. For ocean travel, they use large, hardy vessels, equipped with both sails and anbaric engines. Lyra travels aboard the King of the Gyptians' ship, the *Noorderlicht*, from Brytain to the port of Trollesund in Norroway.

Sledges (above) are the main form of transportation in the Arctic.

Used by the Magisterium to track its enemies and retrieve objects, the spy-fly is a clockwork, insect-like creation from the continent of Afric. The spy fly's mechanisms are powered by an evil spirit trapped inside the device.

The Noorderlicht *heads for Norroway (right). The spy-fly (below) is a deadly tool used against Lyra and the Gyptians by the Magisterium.*

The Magisterium

The Magisterium is the organization that governs the world in which Lyra lives. It attempts to control people's lives and to tell them what they should believe in. Lord Asriel's plan to shatter the barrier between the universes threatens the Magisterium – but it also offers the organization an opportunity to conquer and control new worlds. The Magisterium's influence extends far and wide, and its London headquarters are based in an imposing skyscraper known as the Magisterial Seat.

The Magisterium's work is shrouded in secrecy and many people fear the organization. Anyone who disagrees with its views on important matters are accused of heresy, which leads to arrest and often imprisonment. This is the fate that befalls the Master of Jordan College after he grants Lord Asriel's request for money for his expedition to the North. The Magisterium also controls a powerful police force. In less developed areas, the Magisterium uses hired help to enforce its will. In the North, it employs ruthless Tartar warriors and fearsome armoured Ice Bears.

The Magisterial police are a highly trained, military-style organization. Its officers obey the orders of the Magisterium without question.

Magisterial police storm the halls of Jordan College to arrest the Master for heresy (left). Standing to attention, the police await orders from Fra Pavel (centre). In the North, Tartar warriors guard the Magisterium's Experimental Station, also known as Bolvangar (right).

Fra Pavel is a senior figure in the Magisterium. Sly and ruthless, Pavel holds the rank of Commissar. His dæmon takes the form of a chameleon, a lizard that can change colour to hide itself. Fra Pavel is determined to stop Lord Asriel and his plans for a further expedition to the North. First, he tries to force the Master of Jordan College to stop Lord Asriel. When the Master refuses, Pavel attempts to poison Asriel by slipping a packet of white powder into a decanter full of '99 Tokay, one of Asriel's favourite wines. Lyra's intervention foils this plot, and Pavel is incensed when Asriel is granted the money he needs for his trip. Shortly after Asriel leaves for the North, the Master is arrested. Fra Pavel questions him to find the whereabouts of Asriel's alethiometer, which he knows has been at Jordan College for many years. But the Master, who has secretly bequeathed the device to Lyra, gives nothing away.

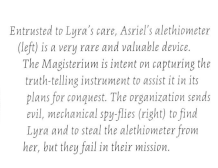

Entrusted to Lyra's care, Asriel's alethiometer (left) is a very rare and valuable device. The Magisterium is intent on capturing the truth-telling instrument to assist it in its plans for conquest. The organization sends evil, mechanical spy-flies (right) to find Lyra and to steal the alethiometer from her, but they fail in their mission.

The Gobblers

In the cities of Oxford and London, children have been disappearing. Some believe they are being kidnapped and eaten alive, while others say the children have been taken down to Hell. But the truth is even more sinister – they are being snatched by hired child-catchers who work for a shady organization called the General Oblation Board, or G.O.B. for short. Ordinary people, hearing of the G.O.B.'s activities and fearing for the safety of their own children, have another name for the organization's agents – the Gobblers.

To the children of Oxford, the Gobblers are a terrifying but fascinating threat. Stories about the Gobblers are rife, and Lyra has heard many tales about children disappearing. One such victim is Jessie Reynolds, the niece of Jordan College's housekeeper, Mrs Lonsdale. Lyra and her best friend, Roger Parslow, promise each other that if either of them is kidnapped, the other will come to their rescue. But when Lyra leaves Jordan College to go to London with Mrs Coulter, she is unaware that Roger has become the Gobblers' latest victim.

Roger (above) wanders through the grounds of Jordan College, unaware that he is being followed by the Gobblers.

Fold

Bend back

KING OF THE GYPTIANS

THE MODERN WORLD

AERONAUT FOR HIRE

The Golden Monkey

Mrs. Coulter

[ä·lē·thē·ä·meter]
Alethiometer
– from "aletheia", the Greek word for truth. By pointing at three symbols you can ask any question you can imagine.

NORTHERN ANBARIC COMPANY

PANSERBJØRNE
IOREK
WHO IS YOUR KING?

QUEEN OF THE WITCH CLAN

NOORDERLIGHT

When the Gobblers pursue Lyra in London's Wharflands, they capture her in a net. Their success is brief – they soon meet a swift end in a hail of well-aimed Gyptian arrows.

In London, Lyra becomes suspicious of Mrs Coulter. Her elegant appearance hides a ruthless and bullying nature, and this prompts Lyra and Pan to search her study. But they find more than they bargained for when they discover papers that reveal Mrs Coulter is in charge of the General Oblation Board. Shortly after this, Mrs Coulter's monkey-dæmon tries to steal the alethiometer, forcing Lyra and Pan to run away from Mrs Coulter's luxurious apartment.

GENERAL OBLATION BOARD
Restricted Material

Lost on the streets of London, Lyra is nearly captured by Gobblers hired by Mrs Coulter to find her. She is saved by the intervention of the Gyptians (pgs 28–29). When Lyra learns that Roger has been kidnapped, she joins the Gyptians on their quest to rescue all of the children abducted by the General Oblation Board.

The Gyptians learn from the witch Serafina Pekkala (pgs 34–35) that the Gobblers' victims have been taken to a research station known as Bolvangar (pgs 40-41). But on the way to Bolvangar, Lyra makes a shocking discovery. In a remote trapper's hut, she encounters Billy Costa, a Gyptian boy she knows from Oxford. Billy has escaped from the Gobblers, but something terrible has happened to him – he has lost his dæmon...

With his dæmon missing, Billy Costa is sick, weak and barely able to walk (top and bottom right).

Lyra's London

Although Lyra is used to living in a city, life in Oxford cannot prepare her for the wonders she sees in the far larger metropolis of London. She travels with Mrs Coulter from Oxford to London onboard a Magisterial sky ferry, which provides Lyra with an amazing aerial tour of the sprawling city which is about to become her new home.

Perched beside the window of the sky ferry with Pan, Lyra is astounded at the size of London and its major landmarks. Skyscrapers linked by glass-covered walkways tower up into the sky, hundreds of metres from the ground, while the River Thames winds its way through the city. Awe-inspiring Magisterial offices are spread throughout the metropolis, and there are many elegant parks and gardens.

When Lyra arrives at Mrs Coulter's apartment she is even more excited. The spacious building has an impressive sweeping staircase in the entrance hall, and its furnishings and decorations are graceful and feminine – just like Mrs Coulter. Lyra gets a spacious, beautiful bedroom of her own, as well as a whole wardrobe full of pretty new clothes.

Mrs Coulter points out the sights of London to Lyra from the observation deck of the Magisterial sky ferry.

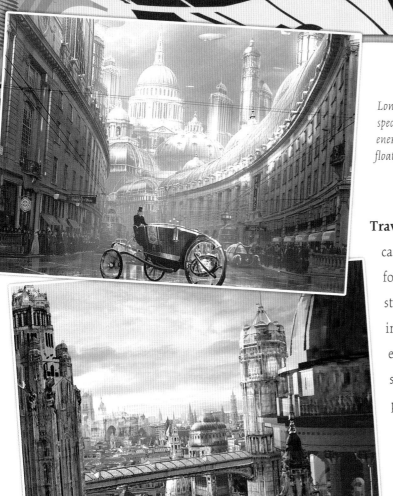

London, the capital of Lyra's Brytain, is a truly spectacular city. Taxis powered by glowing anbaric energy speed through its busy streets, while airships float overhead above the city's towering spires.

Travelling around London in an anbaric-powered carriage, the city's wealth and grandeur is clear for Lyra to see, with its broad promenades, large stone buildings and sweeping arcades. Lyra's life in London is a blur of engagements. She dines in expensive restaurants, meets powerful people and socializes with wealthy ladies. Mrs Coulter even pampers her with beauty treatments. However, Mrs Coulter's promise to train Lyra and take her to the North fails to materialize. And one night, after Mrs Coulter's monkey-dæmon tries to steal the alethiometer, Lyra and Pan flee the apartment.

Wandering at night, the streets of London no longer seem so welcoming. Lyra finds herself in a dimly lit area of markets and docks known as the Wharflands. Drifting through the streets, Lyra suddenly finds herself pursued by the Gobblers – sinister child-kidnappers (below). Fortunately for Lyra, the Gobblers are not the only people that are following her, and help is close at hand...

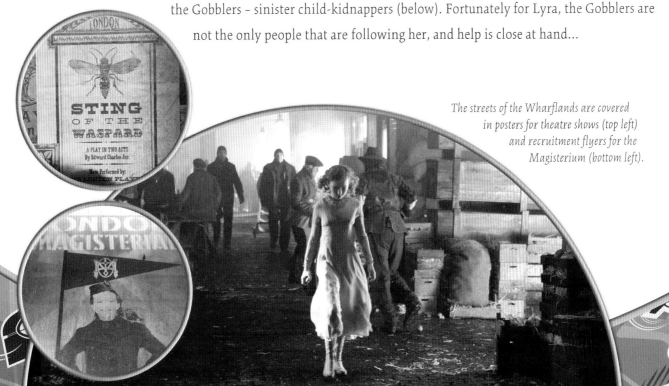

The streets of the Wharflands are covered in posters for theatre shows (top left) and recruitment flyers for the Magisterium (bottom left).

The Gyptians

After Lyra escapes from Mrs Coulter's London home, she is attacked by the Gobblers – thugs that kidnap unaccompanied children for mysterious purposes. But she is rescued by the Gyptians, a group of sea-faring warriors and traders who have been watching her every move ever since she left the safety of Oxford.

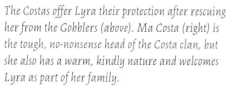

The Gyptians are the far-flung descendants of a race from the east who travelled to all the corners of the globe. They live on houseboats, barges and ships moored on rivers and canals. A proud, loyal and honest people, the Gyptians have suffered greatly at the hands of the sinister Gobblers. Pooling their fighting men and wealth in order to mount an expedition to the North, the Gyptians hope to recover all of their own stolen children as well as children belonging to "landloper" families.

The Costas offer Lyra their protection after rescuing her from the Gobblers (above). Ma Costa (right) is the tough, no-nonsense head of the Costa clan, but she also has a warm, kindly nature and welcomes Lyra as part of her family.

Gyptians are found all over
Lyra's world. Tribes are
identified by their clothing
and types of tattoos (below).

The Costas are a family of Gyptians that Lyra and her best friend, Roger Parslow,
know in Oxford. They belong to a tribe called the Western Gyptians of Fens of
Eastanglia. The head of the family is Ma Costa, a powerful, formidable woman.
In Oxford, Lyra and Roger are both friendly with Billy Costa, the youngest boy in
the family. When Lyra leaves Jordan with Mrs Coulter, Ma Costa – suspicious of the
elegant Magisterial agent's motives – decides to take action. Tracking Lyra's every move,
the Costas arrive just in time to save her from joining the Gobblers' victims.

Lyra travels with the Costas on their barge as they sail out to sea to dock with
a larger ship called the *Noorderlicht*. Here Lyra meets John Faa – the King of the
Gyptians. She soon discovers that both Billy Costa and Roger Parslow have been
kidnapped and taken to the North. Ma Costa is eventually reunited with her son
Billy – but he is half the boy she once knew...

*Ma Costa comforts her son Billy, who
has lost his dæmon (left).*

*John Faa listens to a Gyptian
spy's dying words on the deck of
the Noorderlicht (left).*

29

John Faa

John Faa is the King of the Gyptians. He is their undisputed leader, and has the respect of all the Gyptian clans and families. When Gyptian children start to disappear, he calls together the six Gyptian tribes for a gathering on his ship, the Noorderlicht. His spies have discovered that the children have been taken to the North, and he unites the tribes on a rescue mission. Faa has seen many battles and is growing old in years, but his power to inspire people and strike fear into the hearts of his enemies still remains.

John Faa's dæmon is a crow, and like her human, she is courageous, curious and swift to act. Faa's dæmon saves Lyra when she is attacked by one of the Magisterium's deadly spy-flies. The Gyptian leader is concerned for Lyra's safety, but he is impressed by her bravery and determination. Faa decides to allow her to travel with his Gyptian warriors, and they head north aboard the *Noorderlicht*. Sailing along the coast of Norroway, they dock at the busy port of Trollesund.

Lyra is awestruck when she first meets the mighty John Faa (below), but he is equally won over by her strength of character.

John Faa is a veteran of many battles and campaigns. His trusty revolver has seen action in many battles.

Faa's physical strength and massive size make him a fearsome opponent in battle. He leads from the front, and is unconcerned with his own safety if he can protect the lives of others. When the Gyptians move on from Trollesund, their camp is attacked and he is wounded by an arrow during the battle. Despite his injury, he leads the Gyptian raid on the mysterious experimental station at Bolvangar, where the kidnapped children are being held.

KING OF THE GYPTIANS

In the cabin of the Noorderlicht, John Faa plans his strategy for rescuing the children from the clutches of the Gobblers. Using a detailed map (right), he is able to plot the fastest route by sea to the northern port of Trollesund. He also has a curious nature, and is spellbound by the workings of Lyra's alethiometer.

Farder Coram

Kind, gentle and wise, Farder Coram is counsellor to John Faa, King of the Gyptians. He is an important and highly respected part of the Gyptians' leadership. Coram is old and quite frail, and relies on a long wooden staff to help him when walking. Despite his ageing body, his mind is sharp and his eyes burn with intelligence. He is an amazing source of knowledge on many different subjects.

From the moment they meet aboard John Faa's ship, Lyra and Farder Coram form a bond of mutual respect and understanding. Coram cannot read the alethiometer himself, but he advises Lyra not to grasp for an answer too hard and instead to keep a question in her mind "like it was something alive". When a spy-fly sent to find Lyra and steal the alethiometer is captured, Farder Coram identifies the device and traps it. And when the ship arrives at Trollesund in Norroway, it is Coram who goes with Lyra to convince the Ice Bear, Iorek Byrnison, to join the Gyptian campaign.

Farder Coram's dæmon, Sophonax, takes the form of a cat with beautiful golden fur.

When Serafina Pekkala (left) lands on the deck of John Faa's ship on its way to Trollesund, she asks Lyra to give Farder Coram a sprig of cloud pine as a token of her affection (below left).

Farder Coram was once in love with a beautiful witch called Serafina Pekkala. When Coram was a strong and handsome young man, he saved Serafina when she fell out of the sky. But his heart was broken, as the difference between his short human life and the centuries-long existence of a witch made the relationship impossible.

Exhausted after the Gyptians trek across the ice to help save the children being held at Bolvangar, Farder Coram has to summon all his will power to carry on. But, he still has enough energy to urge Serafina to protect Lyra in the struggles ahead. "Whatever side you choose in what's to come," he says to the witch, "make it Lyra's side."

Farder Coram is fiercely protective of Lyra (above), and would sacrifice his own life to save hers.

Farder Coram's quick action saves Lyra's life when he captures a deadly spy-fly and traps it in a tin (left).

Although he is old, the Gyptian elder is still a crack-shot with his flintlock pistol (above).

Serafina and the Witches

High in the Northern sky, fleeting shadows speed through the air. To the casual observer, they might appear to be a gathering of clouds or a trick of the light. But these black shapes are in fact the witches of the North – long-lived women gifted with amazing powers, including the ability to fly.

Serafina Pekkala is the ethereally beautiful Clan-queen of a group of witches based around Lake Enara in the cold Arctic tundra. Witches live far longer than humans, and Serafina's youthful appearance is deceptive – in fact, she is over 300-years-old. A witch's dæmon can also stray much further than a human's without causing either the witch or her dæmon pain or discomfort. Serafina's dæmon, Kaisa, takes the form of a snow goose.

The witches believe in a prophecy that warns of a coming war that will decide the fate of all the worlds in every universe. A child will play a great part in the outcome of this great battle, and Serafina Pekkala believes that Lyra is this child. The witch visits Lyra one night as she travels with the Gyptians to Trollesund aboard the *Noorderlicht*. She tells Lyra that the children captured by the Gobblers are being held at a place called Bolvangar. She also hands Lyra a spray of cloud pine – the witches' sacred tree – to give to Farder Coram. Over 50 years ago Serafina was in love with Coram, but their love was doomed; she kept her beauty and energy, while he grew old and infirm. Despite the impossibility of their relationship, she still has strong feelings for the Gyptian elder.

Like all witches, Serafina is at one with nature. This gives her the ability to withstand the extreme cold of the North without the need for warm clothing.

When Serafina lands on the deck of the *Noorderlicht*, she tests Lyra's skill with the alethiometer. The witch asks Lyra to use the device to tell her which of the men on the ship was once her lover. When the alethiometer reveals the answer to be Farder Coram, it confirms to Serafina that Lyra has a special ability to read the truth-telling instrument.

Serafina is unsure which side the witches will take in the coming conflict. She tells Lyra that the next time they meet it might be as enemies or as friends. With that, she flies off into the night.

Witches are deadly shots, firing lethal arrows from bows made of cloud pine.

When the pair meet again, it is as allies. Serafina leads a group of witches who defend Lyra and the kidnapped children from the Tartars as they escape from Bolvangar. As the witches' arrows rain down on the enemy soldiers, Lyra, Iorek and Roger Parslow escape in Lee Scoresby's airship (pgs 36–37). Serafina rides alongside and talks to Lee as the airship travels towards the kingdom of Svalbard.

QUEEN OF THE WITCH CLAN

Aboard Lee Scoresby's airship, Serafina and the aeronaut discuss the witches' prophecy about the coming war.

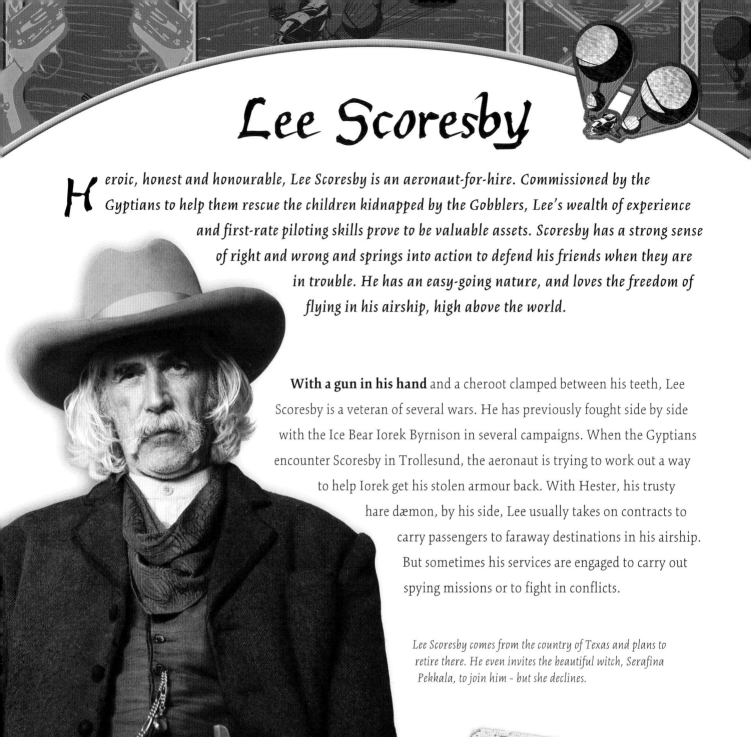

Lee Scoresby

Heroic, honest and honourable, Lee Scoresby is an aeronaut-for-hire. Commissioned by the Gyptians to help them rescue the children kidnapped by the Gobblers, Lee's wealth of experience and first-rate piloting skills prove to be valuable assets. Scoresby has a strong sense of right and wrong and springs into action to defend his friends when they are in trouble. He has an easy-going nature, and loves the freedom of flying in his airship, high above the world.

With a gun in his hand and a cheroot clamped between his teeth, Lee Scoresby is a veteran of several wars. He has previously fought side by side with the Ice Bear Iorek Byrnison in several campaigns. When the Gyptians encounter Scoresby in Trollesund, the aeronaut is trying to work out a way to help Iorek get his stolen armour back. With Hester, his trusty hare dæmon, by his side, Lee usually takes on contracts to carry passengers to faraway destinations in his airship. But sometimes his services are engaged to carry out spying missions or to fight in conflicts.

Lee Scoresby comes from the country of Texas and plans to retire there. He even invites the beautiful witch, Serafina Pekkala, to join him – but she declines.

Lee Scoresby's airship is more than just the tool of his trade - it's his passport to freedom. He cherishes it and looks after it very carefully. Twin balloons filled with hydrogen gas keep the airship aloft, while anbaric engines at the rear of the cockpit drive the airship forward.

When Lee meets Lyra and the Gyptians in Trollesund, he suggests that Iorek Byrnison would make a good ally. Knowing that Iorek has lost his armour and fallen on hard times, the wily aeronaut hopes that the prospect of a campaign will help to restore the Ice Bear's dignity and fighting spirit.

When Iorek discovers that his stolen armour is being held at the Magisterial office in Trollesund, he breaks into the building to reclaim it. The Magisterial guards stand ready to shoot the rampaging Ice Bear. But their captain backs down when a pistol is pointed at his own head. The man holding the gun is Iorek's old comrade-in-arms - Lee Scoresby.

Lee's hare-dæmon, Hester, is as cool under fire as Scoresby himself. Her keen hearing has saved the aeronaut's life on many occasions.

Iorek Byrnison

Banished from his home kingdom of Svalbard, the Ice Bear known as Iorek Byrnison is employed at the sledge depot behind Einarsson's Bar in Trollesund. The brooding, terrifying figure was once a Panserbjørne – an armoured warrior whose sole purpose was to fight in battles and wars. But Iorek has lost his armour, which he considers to be part of his soul, and so he remains in Trollesund. The arrival of the Gyptians, and their offer of paid work to fight in a campaign, marks a change in the Ice Bear's fortunes.

A highly skilled metalworker, Iorek works in Trollesund fixing broken machines and mending objects made out of iron. In return, he is given large chunks of reindeer meat to eat and jugs of whisky to drink. Iorek's giant face rarely shows any emotion, except when he is snarling or roaring in anger.

Iorek was defeated in combat in Svalbard by the bear-king Ragnar Sturlusson and, as a result, sent into exile. Wandering through the frozen North, Iorek ended up in Trollesund. The terrified townspeople got him drunk on spirits, then stole and hid his armour while he was sleeping. Without his armour, Iorek cannot go to war, which is what Panserbjørne do most. Nor can he make a new set, as an Ice Bear's armour is made from tough sky-iron that can only be found in the falling stars that land in Svalbard.

When Lyra and Farder Coram first meet Iorek he is employed as a metal-worker near Einarsson's bar (left) in Trollesund.

A fully armoured Iorek (right) bursts through the doors of the Magisterial offices in Trollesund.

When the Gyptians try to hire Iorek, Lyra uses the alethiometer to locate his stolen armour. The amazed Ice Bear swiftly retrieves the armour from the local Magisterial offices, and declares he is in debt to Lyra. Joining the Gyptians on their quest to rescue the children kidnapped by the Gobblers, Iorek becomes Lyra's loyal and trusted friend. Their adventures lead them to Svalbard, where Iorek finally has a rematch with his old enemy, Ragnar Sturlusson.

Iorek's armour is crude, battered and rusty (left), but when he is wearing it the Ice Bear looks absolutely terrifying. Without his armour, Iorek feels that part of his soul is missing - like a human without their dæmon. But with it, he is once again a mighty Panserbjørne - a formidable foe to his enemies but utterly loyal and dependable to those he serves.

PANSERBJØRNE

"IOREK!

WHO IS YOUR KING?

Bolvangar

In the far North there lies a place where no birds fly, and from which all animals have fled. The witches call it "Bolvangar" – the place of fear. It is the name given to the General Oblation Board's Experimental Station. Pounded by fierce winds and blizzards, its low, white buildings are guarded by fierce Tartars and their wolf-dæmons. Bolvangar is the final destination for the children kidnapped by the Gobblers – one of whom is Lyra's friend, Roger Parslow. The children are given rooms and toys to play with, and the dining hall is decorated in bright, cheerful colours, but this is a far from happy place.

Lyra's encounter with Billy Costa (pg 25) confirms her worst fears about the secret purpose of the General Oblation Board. She reunites Billy with his mother, Ma Costa, but shortly afterwards the Gyptians are attacked by Samoyeds – local trappers in the pay of the Magisterium. In the confusion, Lyra is kidnapped and taken to Bolvangar. The officials who run the station have no idea who Lyra is, and she tells them that her name is Lizzie Brooks. She is soon reunited with her old friend Roger and meets many other children who have also been brought to the station. They have been told that they need an operation to avoid illness, but the truth is far more sinister.

The Experimental Station hides a grim secret – the intercision machine (below).

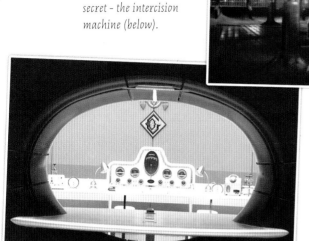

Deep inside Bolvangar, there is a guarded room with a soundproof door, so that no one outside can hear the screams. Inside this chilling place stands a machine with two cage-like compartments – one is for a child and the other for its dæmon. Above the cage looms a terrifying, anbaric-powered guillotine. This machine is used to cut the bond of energy between a child and their dæmon – an operation that was performed upon Billy Costa. The General Oblation Board believes that particles from space called Dust, which flow into adults through their dæmons, gives people bad ideas. By cutting the link between a human and their dæmon before puberty, the G.O.B. believes they can stop people becoming contaminated by Dust. This horrifying operation is called intercision.

When Mrs Coulter arrives at Bolvangar, Lyra hides from her. But Lyra is soon captured by Bolvangar staff, who are unaware of her connection with the glamorous head of the G.O.B. The staff force Lyra and Pan into the intercision cages; the horror of being separated from her beloved Pan is too much and Lyra passes out. Fortunately for Lyra, a shocked Mrs Coulter walks in on the operation, just in time to stop Lyra and Pan being separated for ever. Before long, Lyra stages a breakout, leading Roger and the other children to freedom as the Gyptians, the witches, Iorek and Lee Scoresby arrive to help fight off the Tartar guards.

Terrified at the prospect of intercision, Lyra and Pan desperately try to escape from the machine's cage-like compartments (left). Mrs Coulter (above) arrives just in time to save them from the intercision procedure.

Svalbard

$\mathcal{D}$uring the battle at Bolvangar, Lyra, Roger and Iorek jump aboard Lee Scoresby's airship. They head for Svalbard, the kingdom of the Ice Bears. Lyra plans to free Lord Asriel, who is being held prisoner there. But they are caught in a blizzard, and Lyra falls out of the airship over Svalbard. She lands safely, but is captured by some sentry bears, who take her to the bear-king's palace.

Built of marble and ice, the palace is heavily guarded. Its ramparts are lined with armoured bears, who stand ready to fire their deadly flame-hurlers at approaching enemies. Designed to be the grandest palace imaginable, it is in fact an ugly hotch-potch of different building styles. Lyra is taken through the main gates and into a giant hall, littered with the rotting carcasses of dead seals and splattered with bird droppings. There she meets the cunning, vicious ruler of the Ice Bears – King Ragnar Sturlusson.

The Ice Bears of Svalbard – also known as Panserbjørne – stand guard over King Ragnar's palace (below). Their tough armour is made from sky-iron found in the falling stars that land on Svalbard.

*Ragnar's magnificent armour (right) makes
the huge bear appear even more terrifying.*

Ragnar is the unchallenged ruler of Svalbard.
Even more massive than Iorek Byrnison, he
poisoned the previous king and then beat Iorek
– the heir to the crown – in single-handed combat.
The bear-king is decorated in jewels and his
long claws are covered in gold.

Lyra knows that Iorek will come looking for her, but
that when he arrives at Svalbard he will be killed by the
sentry bears. She convinces Ragnar that Iorek has managed to
acquire the one thing the bear-king himself desperately wants – his
own dæmon. Lyra persuades him that she is Iorek's dæmon, but that she
wants to be joined with Ragnar. She tells the bear-king that the only way to do
this is for Ragnar to defeat Iorek in single combat. When Iorek arrives – with Roger on
his back – Lyra explains the situation. The mighty Ice Bear is very pleased at the chance of a rematch,
and even gives Lyra a new name in honour of her story-telling abilities – "Lyra Silvertongue".

The battle is brutal and ferocious. The ground shudders as the two huge bears collide. Iorek suffers a bad neck
wound and appears to be limping badly. Poised for victory, Ragnar taunts his exhausted adversary. But suddenly
Iorek powers upwards and with a mighty swipe of a huge paw, strikes out at Ragnar. Within moments, Ragnar is
dead. The bears of Svalbard are stunned into silence, but when Iorek asks them, "Who is your king?" they roar and
answer as one – "Iorek Byrnison!"

*Seated on his throne, King Ragnar surveys the vast Grand
Hall of his palace (left). The Ice Bears gather to watch as the
fight between Iorek and Ragnar begins (below).*

The Gateway to Other Worlds

After Iorek's victory at Svalbard, Lyra and Roger are shown to the prison quarters of Lord Asriel. Instead of a cold, damp cell, the explorer's rooms are luxurious and Asriel has been allowed to continue with his experiments. After talking with Asriel about his plans, Lyra and Roger go to sleep in a spare room. But when Lyra awakes, she discovers that Roger and Lord Asriel have gone. Consulting the alethiometer, she calls for Iorek and they set off across the ice in pursuit.

Lyra and Iorek pound across the ice, but they soon encounter a deep gap in the icy ground. A narrow bridge of ice juts out across the divide, but it is too fragile to withstand Iorek's weight. After a tearful farewell, Lyra crosses the bridge alone. She soon catches sight of Asriel and Roger. Lyra watches from a distance as Asriel unloads an intricate piece of machinery from his sledge and attaches Roger to it with a long cable. As he does so, Asriel's powerful snow-leopard dæmon, Stelmaria, holds Roger's dæmon tightly between her jaws.

On Asriel's earlier expedition to the North Pole, the ghostly outline of a city could be seen in the sky. When Asriel breaks the barrier between the universes, Lyra walks through the gateway he has created into this mysterious city in another world.

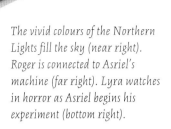

The vivid colours of the Northern Lights fill the sky (near right). Roger is connected to Asriel's machine (far right). Lyra watches in horror as Asriel begins his experiment (bottom right).

On his previous expedition to the North, Asriel saw the particles known as Dust flow from the sky into a person's dæmon. But unlike Mrs Coulter and the General Oblation Board – who are concerned with the effect of Dust on people's behaviour – Asriel is interested in the particles as a powerful form of energy. By tapping into the energy, he believes he can break the barrier between the universes.

Horrified, Lyra can only watch helplessly as Asriel triggers his machine. Roger's dæmon is destroyed in a vast blaze of energy that arcs across the sky, tearing it open and creating a vast gateway to other worlds. Lyra looks for Roger but he has disappeared. Suddenly, Mrs Coulter arrives and Asriel asks her to come with him to a new world, but she refuses his request. Lyra is filled with hatred for both of them, appalled by their selfishness, cruelty and disregard for the lives of others.

Mrs Coulter and Asriel (above) come face-to-face at the North Pole.

As the ice under their feet breaks up, Asriel strides boldly through the hole he has created in the sky. Mrs Coulter commands Lyra to stay with her, but they are separated as the ice cracks between them. Taking a deep breath, Lyra and Pan step through the gateway into another world...

Asriel's machine (left) harnesses and releases the power of the Dust contained in Roger's dæmon.

ACKNOWLEDGMENTS

Scholastic Children's Books would like to thank everyone at
Scholastic Media and New Line Cinema for their help in the creation of this
book. Special thanks go to the following: Deborah Forte for all her help and
assistance; Tom Fickling and Helen Appleby for their outstanding hospitality
and efficiency; John Mayo for processing our numerous picture requests; Bapty
and Co. for supplying John Faa's revolver and Farder Coram's flintlock pistol;
Jason Cox for his design assistance.

Photography by Laurie Sparham

Additional photography by Michelle Martinoli: spy-fly (pgs 4 & 21),
spirit projector (pg 20), sledge (pg 21), John Faa's revolver (pg 31),
Farder Coram's flintlock pistol (pg 33), cloud pine bow and
arrows (pg 35), Asriel's machine (pg 45)

Additional editorial content by Neil Kelly